Soar
Like Eagles

Deepen Your Understanding of
Truth and Find Rest for Your
Soul as You Journal in Layers

MATT PAVLIK
BRINGING YOUR POTENTIAL TO LIGHT

Christian Concepts
Centerville, Ohio

SOAR LIKE EAGLES
Copyright © 2020 by Matt Pavlik.

All rights reserved. No part of this book may be used or reproduced in any manner whatsoever without written permission except in the case of brief quotations embodied in critical articles or reviews.

Published in the United States of America by Christian Concepts (christianconcepts.com), an imprint of New Reflections Counseling, Inc. (newreflectionscounseling.com).

Although the author is a professional counselor, this book is not intended to be a replacement for professional counseling.

April 2020: first edition.

September 2021: minor corrections.

REL012150 RELIGION / Christian Living / Devotional Journal

Pavlik, Matthew Edward, 1971-
Soar Like Eagles / Matt Pavlik.

ISBN: 978-1-951866-00-6 (softcover)

1. Spiritual journals—Authorship—Religious aspects—Christianity
2. Diaries—Authorship—Religious aspects—Christianity

Journaling, Hope, Healing, Growth, Self-acceptance, Meaning (Philosophy), Rejection (Psychology), Self-deception

Scripture quotations marked NLT are taken from the Holy Bible, New Living Translation, copyright © 1996, 2004, 2015 by Tyndale House Foundation. Used by permission of Tyndale House Publishers, Inc., Carol Stream, Illinois 60188. All rights reserved.

Scripture quotations marked (NIV) are taken from the Holy Bible, New International Version®, NIV®. Copyright © 1973, 1978, 1984, 2011 by Biblica, Inc.™ Used by permission of Zondervan. All rights reserved worldwide. www.zondervan.com. The "NIV" and "New International Version" are trademarks registered in the United States Patent and Trademark Office by Biblica, Inc.™

Scripture quotations marked ESV are from the ESV® Bible (The Holy Bible, English Standard Version®), copyright © 2001 by Crossway Bibles, a publishing ministry of Good News Publishers. Used by permission. All rights reserved.

IMAGES

Cover: PxHere: 747075

Introduction: pixabay - Gellinger: 3065387; Skeeze: 899055, 3953305; Clker-Free-Vector-Images: 25737, 32249; mohamed_hassan: 3266163; OpenClipart-Vectors: 153278

Chapter #01: pixabay - Free-Photos: 690104

Chapter #02: freeimages - Katherine Evans: Broken Mirror; Free-Photos: 802099

Chapter #03:

Chapter #04:

Chapter #05: pixabay - Kanenori: 2124113

Chapter #06: pixabay - OpenClipart-Vectors: 158714

Chapter #07: weezieworks.com - Louise Waller: Snuggle

Chapter #08: weezieworks.com - Louise Waller: Mountains of Praise

Chapter #09: pixabay - waldryano: 1668636

Chapter #10:

Chapter #11: pixabay - OpenClipart-Vectors: 147190

Chapter #12: Matt Pavlik: Capstone

Chapter #13: pixabay - Manuchi: 3310319

Chapter #14:

CONTENTS

Introduction: Do You Want To Soar? 1
Chapter #01: Layer #1 What Blocks Your Life Goal? 7
Chapter #02: Why Journal? 9
Chapter #03: How To Journal 13
Chapter #04: Technique #1: Story 15
Chapter #05: Layer #2 Explore Your Story 17
Chapter #06: Technique #2: Stream of Thought 19
Chapter #07: Technique #3: Prompts 21
Chapter #08: Layer #3: Overcome Obstacles 25
Chapter #09: Technique #4: Prayer 27
Chapter #10: Technique #5: Emotional Expression 29
Chapter #11: Layer #4: Lament Your Struggle 31
Chapter #12: Technique #6: Drawing 33
Chapter #13: Layer #5: Draw a Symbol 35
Chapter #14: Continue to Journal in Layers 37

Introduction

Do You Want To Soar?

*But those who hope in the LORD
will renew their strength.
They will soar on wings like eagles;
they will run and not grow weary,
they will walk and not be faint.*

—Isaiah 40:31 NIV

It rained some but I'm not sure if I'm going home. When I was 10 years old, I wrote those words on a notepad while I sat on my bicycle at a park about 5 miles from my home.

Those words are etched in my memory today, almost 40 years later, probably because I wrote them down. They're part of my story. Story is one of six journaling techniques that will help you soar.

I started journaling (for real) when I was 20 years old. I continue to use it today. Along with personal counseling it's the most important tool I have to better my life.

MATT PAVLIK

As a counselor, I've seen my clients' faces brighten during an a-ha moment in our sessions. Likewise, their faces are brighter after they return from a time of journaling. During their flashes of insight, various unassociated pieces of information come together, giving them greater understanding.

Finding insight requires effort. When clients first come in they are usually confused, hurting, and disorganized. All the uncomfortable feelings accumulate inside until they are released.

What happens if you keep filling a balloon? Eventually it pops. What happens if you internalize experiences but never process them? You pop. Have you ever been around a person when they "pop"? Journaling makes the subconscious, conscious. It lets the air out of the balloon in a controlled way. God doesn't want you to explode and make a mess all over the place. He wants you to soar.

What Is Soaring?

Soaring is living the all-consuming, spiritual-growth adventure God has in store for you. Soaring isn't for the faint of heart. The ground is a calmer and often saner, but more tedious choice.

Soaring freely through the open sky is a much smoother way to travel. The wind does you little good on the ground. But in the air, you can soar like an eagle.

You can't soar every minute of your life. Even an eagle doesn't spend its whole life in the air. To be successful at soaring you need to be patient with preparing. This means spending time running, walking, and sometimes even crawling.

Soar Like Eagles

Crawl Before You Soar

Journaling builds insight from self-awareness to understanding to meaning. Think of your emotional health in four levels of increasing functioning:
1. You **crawl** when you lack awareness.
2. You **walk** when you become self-aware of your past.
3. You **run** when you understand your identity.
4. You **soar** when you find meaning that leads to action.

Crawl

Crawling represents a severely emotionally broken person. The person's internal state is disorganized and stressed.

Walk With Self-Awareness

Walking represents the ability to tune-in to your experiences. If you want to mature emotionally, you must make contact with what is inside of you. You must experience your thoughts and feelings. When you journal you translate your raw feelings into words, thoughts, and ideas (even if you never say them out loud).

What do you look like inside? Are you clean? Messy? Empty? Shameful? Disgusting? Stuffed?

Run With Understanding

Running represents the ability to sort truth from falsehood. You are able to organize what you've found and look at it through an objective perspective, such as the truth found in the Bible. You'll have substantial answers to questions like: Who am I really? Who does God say I am? What is treasure and what is trash? Refine your self-image by emphasizing what is true about you and discarding what is false.

Soar With Meaning

Soaring represents an emotionally whole person who is able to make wise decisions. Your internal state is ordered and calm. You apply what you are aware of and what you understand. Your see your purpose and have a working idea of what God has planned for you to accomplish. You're ready to act on the plan.

The Secret to Soaring
(How to Journal in Layers)

The secret to soaring in life is to persist in discovering who God is as well as who He made you to be. But what can you do if all you can muster is a crawl? What if your life feels on hold?

To move forward you need an epiphany—that moment when you understand something more clearly than you ever have. An epiphany will permanently change your life. In spiritual terms, epiphany refers to the manifestation of Jesus Christ in your life. The Holy Spirit is responsible for creating epiphanies in your life.

The "journal-in-layers" method I developed encourages epiphanies. Waiting on God allows you to look at your same words, Bible verses, and other ideas with fresh eyes. Then you occupy yourself with other activities and return to see what has changed.

You'll gain more from your journaling experience when you journal in layers. Journaling in layers has four steps:

1. **Represent:** communicate what is internal or subconscious by expressing it in some external or explicit medium (words, symbols, sculptures).
2. **Rest:** acknowledge what you expressed, then wait. Let it simmer, percolate, steep. Introduce a different experience into your life and allow time for change.
3. **Review:** revisit what you expressed, taking it back in and looking for understanding and meaning.
4. **Repeat:** return to step 1.

Revisiting previous writing helps you move from self-awareness to understanding and then to meaning. When you have enough confidence in your understanding, you act. But the process never ends because new experiences often increase the internal disorder.

Continue by integrating your new experiences with the old. Start again at self-awareness and write about what you currently know. Repeat this until you are ready to act. As you build insight and understanding your confidence in God will increase.

The purpose of this book is to introduce you to this method and give you practice using all four steps. Chapters with "Layer" in the title are one of five hands-on exercises.

Chapter 1

Layer #1
What Blocks Your Life Goal?

*Commit your actions to the LORD,
and your plans will succeed.*

*We can make our plans,
but the Lord determines our steps.*

*We may throw the dice,
but the Lord determines how they fall.*

—Proverbs 16:3, 9, 33 NLT

In the picture on the following page, image you are at the bottom looking up at the highest peak. The top represents your ideal situation, desired future, and God's plan for you. Write about a life goal and any obstacles, limitations, or problems that stand in your way.

MATT PAVLIK

Chapter 2

Why Journal?

Journaling helps you make contact with your emotional life, so you can understand who you are and fulfill God's purposes for your life. Often, the purpose of waiting on the Lord is to grow in acknowledging and accepting your dependence on the Lord.

Experiences can be neutral. Take for example, *I'm standing in line to see Santa Clause.* There's nothing particularly inspiring or discouraging about that. But personal encounters are different—they can be negative or positive.

Negative experiences can be emotionally charged. They can convince you that you are defective when you're really not. *Santa Clause knocked me on the head and stole my wallet. Why would he do that? I must be a bad person.*

Positive experiences can also be emotionally charged. They can convince you of the truth that you are worthwhile.

Santa Clause smiled at me and handed me a gift I've always wanted. Why would he do that? I must be a valuable person.

To thrive in life, you need some way to discount the negatives and believe the positives. The three main obstacles to accomplishing this are a lack of truth, a lack of healing, and a lack of identity. You can overcome these obstacles with spiritual disciplines such as: praying, studying, journaling, fellowshipping, mentoring, and counseling.

Like praying and studying, journaling is a solitary spiritual discipline. You don't need others to participate. The journal-in-layers method encourages you to focus on God's truth, your healing, your identity, and then bold action.

Truth Focused

God's truth is the foundation of all healing. Journaling will be much more effective when you interact with the truth because it helps you understand who God is. The Bible contains the truth but you can use others sources like books, quotes, and art. As you affirm the truth, it helps you:
- Get on the same page with God.
- Deepen your understanding of creation.
- Increase your confidence.

Healing Focused

If you're out of touch with who God made you to be, you might be plagued with feeling "less": useless, worthless, and hopeless.

Your baggage is the accumulation of all your negative interpretations of your life events. Baggage is whatever weighs you down. It's the lies that prevent you from understanding who you really are. It's a belief that you can't shake like, "I'm worthless."

Journaling promotes the healing process because it:
- Prepares your heart so that God can mend your broken, missing-in-action parts into a healthy whole.
- Helps you drop emotional baggage and grow in faith so you are less burdened.
- Increases your capabilities in proportion to the healing you have experienced.

Identity Focused

You might not feel worthless anymore, but do you feel significant? Are you confident in who God made you to be? Negative experiences are extremely common. But after you remove your baggage, you are empty. Nature abhors a vacuum. If you don't fill up with the truth about who you really are, lies will rush in to define you again.

Journaling helps you find and accept your true identity. As you revisit your writing you will be able to:

- Become in touch with who you are from a different perspective.
- Explore your inner world of thoughts and feelings, going beyond a list of tasks to complete.
- Build upon and make sense of your life experiences to see how they inform who God made you to be.

Action Focused

Journaling helps you overcome the obstacles in the way of your goals. Reflecting on your writing prepares you for action because it encourages you to:
- Be aware of your spiritual and emotional growth.
- Understand who you are and fulfill God's plan for your life.
- Develop boldness and determination to reach your desired future.

Chapter 3

How To Journal

Here are three ways to start journaling:
1. Choose the Most Appropriate Means
2. Be as Genuine as You Can
3. Use a Proven Technique

Choose the Most Appropriate Means

The journal-in-layers method provides the overall structure, but how should you get started journaling?

I recommend you use paper and pen whenever possible. Paper and pen are more primal and direct. Think of the big fat crayons kindergarteners use. Making contact with paper enables your brain to produce more creative results than tapping at computer keys. This also allows you to draw and doodle, which are relaxing.

Writing with paper and pen is best for connecting with your deepest parts and emotions, and when you want to draw or doodle. Speaking into a recorder is good for verbalizing and expressing, but it requires more privacy. It's harder to revisit unless you want to listen to the whole recording. Typing at an electronic device is okay when you prefer it over writing and speaking. On the plus side, it's easier to search, read, and store.

Be as Genuine as You Can

Be honest, real, and authentic. All of us keep many thoughts and feelings hidden within us. Giving yourself the permission and space to get in touch with them can be life-giving. Before you begin, affirm your intentions. Bring down your walls. Disarm your defenses. Ask for God's help by saying a simple prayer like: *I really want to know what is going on inside of me.*

Use a Proven Technique

This book covers six writing-enhancing techniques.
1. Story
2. Stream-of-thought
3. Prompts
4. Prayer
5. Emotional Expression
6. Drawing

Chapter 4

Technique #1: Story

In the beginning God created the heavens and the earth.
—Genesis 1:1 NIV

Goal: Tell your story as part of God's story.

God is telling a story. You are part of God's story. A story is more meaningful than plain facts, but to learn from your story, you need to write it first.

Every story has a beginning, middle, and an end. Your self-awareness of your past corresponds to the beginning of your story. Your understanding of your present moment corresponds to the middle. Your ability to act on your purpose corresponds to the end.

The story technique fits with the journal-in-layers method because you have a past to become aware of, a present to understand, and a future to live out with meaning and purpose.

MATT PAVLIK

To tell a story is to acknowledge that life is a journey to a specific destination. You have a destiny. You are changing. The story of who you are is unfolding right before you. Allow it to unfold.

Chapter 5

Layer #2
Explore Your Story

Review what you wrote for Layer #1. Keeping in mind your present-day obstacles, think about a different time in your life when your goals were blocked. Write a portion of your life story as it relates to the roadblock.

MATT PAVLIK

Chapter 6

Technique #2: Stream of Thought

Goal: Transfer what is on the inside to the outside without tampering with the source.

Stream-of-thought writing is a spontaneous, unedited, efficient brain dump. There is little to no structure to this technique. This method provides the most direct access to your inner thoughts. How do you really feel?

Start writing. Stop filtering. Keep on writing. If you have the time, write until there is nothing left to write.

MATT PAVLIK

Chapter 7

Technique #3: Prompts

Goal: Prime the pump with prompts.

There are two main approaches to journaling in layers.
1. Keep the theme of your writing the same while you change techniques. This is what the examples in this book demonstrate.
2. Pick one technique and revisit the original source at a regular interval. Prompts are especially good for this. Respond to the prompt, then return at a regular interval (such as in a day, a week, or a month) to reflect on the prompt and all previous responses. Then, write a new response.

When you want to journal, but don't know where to start, a prompt can prime the pump. You might use a quote or a Bible verse. An inspirational picture works well too.

A. Bible Verses

There is no fear in love. But perfect love drives out fear, because fear has to do with punishment. The one who fears is not made perfect in love.
—1 John 4:18 NIV

One way we can be broken is putting our faith in worldly, temporary things, instead of God. Without God, hope becomes meaningless. Intentional journaling directs your attention toward what matters to God. Scripture is a great way to know what matters because it is God's truth for us.

B. Open-Ended Sentences

An incomplete thought or provocative question can start your thoughts flowing.
- I feel hopeless when…
- If you could change one thing about your life, what would it be?

C. Quotes

Quotes can inspire you as you connect with someone else's experience.

People can't live with change if there's not a changeless core inside them. The key to the ability to change is a changeless sense of who you are, what you are about and what you value.
—Stephen R. Covey

D. Images

Visuals can also stimulate the mind. When you look at this picture, are you more aware of your desires? What feelings are stirred up inside of you?

Snuggle © Louise Waller, 2001

E. Go Deeper With Questions

Use the following questions to deepen the truth in your heart.
- What does the prompt say about God?
- What does the prompt say about me?
- What does it mean to me right now, in my present circumstance?

Chapter 8

Layer #3: Overcome Obstacles

Review what you wrote for Layer #1 and #2. Write about what you see in the picture on the following page (or choose another prompt). Consider how it relates to your struggle to overcome obstacles. Write about what it will be like to achieve your goal.

MATT PAVLIK

Chapter 9

Technique #4: Prayer

Goal: Include God in your expression.

Ask God for wisdom and discernment. Write what you want to say to God. Write with awareness that God is present and listening. Imagine that He is watching over your shoulder with love and concern.

MATT PAVLIK

Chapter 10

Technique #5: Emotional Expression

Goal: Focus on emptying yourself of a specific emotion.

When you're journaling, you might be too focused on the facts and forget to feel the impact of your memories in the present moment. Focus on becoming in touch with your feelings and expressing them in your writing. To do this:
1. Recall a time when you felt angry, sad, or anxious (like when Santa hurt you).
2. Write down the facts about that particular event.
3. Pause to remember, and more importantly, to feel the facts. This is the most important step, so don't skip over it quickly. Wait for your feelings to surface. How did you feel when you realized Santa stole your wallet?
4. Write down what you're feeling.

MATT PAVLIK

Structure Your Expression After a Psalm of Lament

One specific way to get started with emotional expression is by writing a lament. A lament is a heartfelt cry to God; it's a process by which you empty yourself of pain and discomfort so you can be filled with God's presence and feel comfort and hope. Psalm 77 (NIV) is an excellent example:

> *I cried out to God for help;*
> *I cried out to God to hear me.*
>
> *When I was in distress, I sought the Lord;*
> *at night I stretched out untiring hands,*
> *and I would not be comforted.*
>
> *I remembered you, God, and I groaned;*
> *I meditated, and my spirit grew faint.*
>
> *"Will the Lord reject forever?*
> *Will he never show his favor again?*
>
> *Has his unfailing love vanished forever?*
> *Has his promise failed for all time?*
>
> *Then I thought, "To this I will appeal:*
> *the years when the Most High*
> *stretched out his right hand.*
>
> *I will remember the deeds of the Lord;*
> *yes, I will remember your miracles of long ago.*
>
> *Your ways, God, are holy.*
> *What god is as great as our God?*
>
> —Psalm 77:1-3, 7-8, 10-11, 13

Chapter 11

Layer #4: Lament Your Struggle

Review what you wrote in Layer #1, #2, and #3. What are you aware of now that you weren't when you created these three layers? Notice what you are feeling. What does it all mean for you? Write a short lament that digs deeper into your current life struggle.

MATT PAVLIK

Chapter 12

Technique #6: Drawing

Goal: Use images and symbols to represent your inner reality.

Drawing is another way to express what is going on inside of you. An idea might be better expressed as a picture or a symbol. Drawing what is inside your head might lead to a more accurate representation than using words. You could draw with stream-of-thought (otherwise known as doodling).

With respect to your goals, a capstone image can be motivating. A capstone is the final stone placed in a building. It fits like a cap. If you have a large project in progress, seeing the capstone can energize you to continue an otherwise burdensome task. The capstone represents the completed work. While placing brick after brick, you can look at the capstone and be encouraged that one day the final stone will be placed.

You could draw a symbolic capstone as a reminder that God will finish what he started (Philippians 1:6).

God encouraged Zerubbable, "Nothing, not even a mighty mountain, will stand in Zerubbabel's way; it will become a level plain before him! And when Zerubbabel sets the final stone of the Temple in place, the people will shout: 'May God bless it! May God bless it!'"
—Zechariah 4:7 NLT

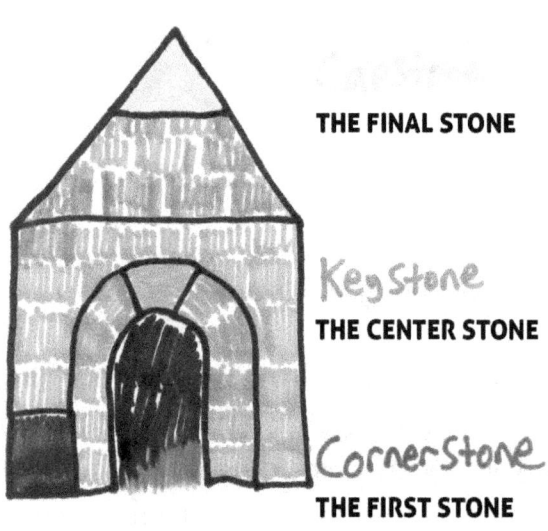

Chapter 13

Layer #5: Draw a Symbol

Review what you wrote in Layer #1, #2, #3, and #4. What does it all mean for you (in your future)? What action can you take as a result of what you've learned today? Action follows naturally from understanding and meaning. If you aren't ready to act, introduce a new prompt or experience and write more.

Like a building, your life is a work in progress. One day your work will end. What do you want the finished product to look like? What image, what capstone, would represent your life and spur you on to finish well?

Doodle or draw a symbol that represents your foundation (your "cornerstone"), what you learned (your "keystone") or what you want to learn (your "capstone").

MATT PAVLIK

Chapter 14

Continue to Journal in Layers

Advanced Journaling

Combine multiple techniques, for example:
- Read a bible verse, pray, and write a lament.
- Tell your life story through pictures.
- Illustrate a Bible verse.

If we "read to know we're not alone" (C.S. Lewis) then we can journal to learn who we are and what God has in store for us.

Journal In Layers

Did you notice how you gained more insight with each layer you completed? The secret to developing truth deeper in your heart is to follow-up with your entries at a regular interval. Here are some other ways you can vary your experience:

MATT PAVLIK

- Change the number of prompts or techniques you cycle through in each layer. You can choose 1 truth and revisit it daily. You could pick 7 prompts and cycle through them weekly.
- Change the time between each cycle. You could explore 7 prompts in one week, but not revisit them for 3 months.
- Change the number of prompts that you study at one time. You could read three separate, but related prompts at the same time, then revisit those same prompts a week or a month later.
- Be flexible. If God is speaking to you through one particular prompt, focus on it for several days.

Have you tried another technique that works for you? Would you like to share how has this book been a blessing to you? Contact me at mpavlik@christianconcepts.com.

Journal Your Way Series

If you like the Journal-in-layers method, try a *Journal Your Way* book. Each one focuses on a core longing (hope, significance, or love) to apply the journal-in-layers method to your devotional life. Visit http://christianconcepts.com/books for details.

ABOUT MATT PAVLIK

Matt Pavlik is a licensed professional clinical counselor who wants each individual restored to their true identity. He completed his Masters in Clinical Pastoral Counseling from Ashland Theological Seminary and his Bachelors in Computer Science from the University of Illinois.

He's been a Christian since 1991 and started journaling around that time. Matt and his wife Georgette have been married since 1999 and live with their four children in Centerville, Ohio.

Blogger

Learn more at ChristianConcepts.com.

Professional Counselor

Matt has more than 15 years of experience counseling individuals and couples at his Christian private practice, New Reflections Counseling (NewReflectionsCounseling.com).

Author

Matt's books help you grow into the person you were made to be. See detailed information at http://christianconcepts.com/books.

Identity Books

To Identity and Beyond demonstrates that the only path to enjoying your life is the journey from where you are at to your place in heaven.

Confident Identity shows you what your identity is and isn't through detailed exercises that culminate in you writing your identity portrait.

Marriage Book

Marriage From Roots To Fruits is a comprehensive workbook with 50 lessons to teach you the techniques to maintain a healthy relationship.

www.ingramcontent.com/pod-product-compliance
Lightning Source LLC
Chambersburg PA
CBHW052127110526
44592CB00013B/1784